Biblical Basis For Healing

RANDY CLARK

Global Awakening
1451 Clark Street
Mechanicsburg, PA 17055

Unless otherwise noted, Scripture quotations are taken from HOLY BIBLE, NEW INTERNATIONAL VERSION®. Copyright © 1973, 1978, 1984 by International Bible Society. Used by permission of Zondervan Publishing House.

First Printing: December 2004

For more information on how to order this book or any of the other materials that Global Awakening offers, please contact:

Global Awakening
1451 Clark Street
Mechanicsburg, PA 17055

1-866-AWAKENING

www.globalawakening.com

Global Awakening
{ Core Message Series }

It is our desire to bring the messages of the Kingdom to the people of God. We have taken what we consider to be core messages from Randy Clark's sermons and schools and printed some of them in booklet form. We hope this teaching increases your understanding of God's purposes for the times we are in and that you find yourself encouraged in your faith. Other core messages are available and they are listed at the end of this booklet.

Table of Contents

{ Introduction }

I was just beginning to learn about words of knowledge when I began to pray for the sick. Because of my lack of faith I didn't often pray for others unless I had a word of knowledge. If I got a word of knowledge for someone, then I could believe for them to get healed. If I didn't have a word of knowledge, then I didn't believe for the healing because I wasn't sure if God wanted to heal that person at that specific time. God was about to teach me a valuable lesson.

In October 1994, almost ten years after my own introduction to the things of the Spirit, I was at the first "Catch the Fire Conference" in Toronto, Canada. It was a large conference – about four or five thousand people.

I felt the Lord say to me, "You hide behind Words of Knowledge. You have to just start saying, 'If you're sick and you're here and you want prayer, I will pray for you.'"

So I went to John Arnott, the senior pastor of the church, and said "John, I think the Lord said I'm supposed to say, 'If anybody's here and you're sick, we'll pray for you tonight.'"

He said, "Randy, do you realize what time we'd get out of here? We wouldn't get out before morning."

"I know John, but I think I'm supposed to do it."

"Ok, if you want to do it, then do it."

So I got up that night and shared with the people what the Lord had laid on my heart. I invited all those who wanted prayer to stay. We were going to pray for them all before we left. There were probably about five to six hundred people that stayed after the meeting to receive prayer.

We started to pray around 10 P.M. and finished at about 4 A.M. I guess that John was wrong; it didn't take all night – just until 4 A.M. That night we saw many people get healed and we had no words of knowledge for them. They were healed by the power of God while we were being obedient to the word that God put on my heart. I have to admit that it took me out of my comfort zone. I was so used to having words of knowledge for healing. This was the first step out of the boat God had me take. He was about to do something in my life.

In 1995, I was at Che Ahn's church in Pasadena, California. I was prepared to preach a certain message that night than the one I actually gave. However, within about five minutes the Lord gave me the thoughts for a new message, and I'm going to share it with you. I wrote down the notes quickly, as the thoughts came to my head. It was so fun! I love it when you get a message from God quickly – that 'rhema' word that just comes together without all the preparation that you have to do for other messages.

The next thing that happened was really scary. The impression came, "As you teach the Word, tell them My anointing will come in their midst, and I will begin to heal them as you are teaching the Word. Tell them when they feel the anointing, to stand up until you see them. Then just say to them, 'I bless you in the Name of Jesus,' or 'God bless you' and then have them sit down."

I thought, "God, what if I say that and You don't do anything? God, I've never seen that done before! That is scary!" I noticed that the Lord got really silent after I said that. I thought to myself: "Is that really God, or is that just me?" Since I was far from St. Louis and wouldn't have to see any of these people again, I decided to go ahead and go for it. I thought to myself that if nothing happened then I would never have to go back to that church again. So I shared this message and the Lord touched many people powerfully that night! Some of them felt heat while others of them felt electricity. Many didn't experience any phenomena at all, but pain began to leave. While I was preaching many stood up, I blessed them in the name of Jesus, and God did His part healing many of them.

The next time I preached this message, I was in Guatemala City to speak in El Shaddai, a church pastored by Harold Cabelleros. The Church then had about 5,000 members. Now it has over 8,000 members. Because of what happened in Pasadena, I prayed silently, "God, can we do that again?" It was strange because He didn't answer me. I took that as a 'YES' from God. Since that time, every time I've preached this message I've given that introduction for people to respond as they feel the anointing come upon them. There has only been one time that I have preached this message that nothing has happened. Every other time I've preached this message God comes and confirms His Word with signs and wonders – especially healings.

Now we are going to go for it again. I believe that as you read this book, many of you are going to feel the anointing of God come upon you, and many of you are going to be healed. What do we have to lose? We have nothing to lose and everything to gain. Somebody could get healed – and today it could even be you!

Jesus said, "Be it done to us according to our faith." What are you expecting from God today?

I do not want to teach you my experience today because my experience falls short of the Word of God. If I taught you my experience, there would be many things that I could not teach because there are a lot of things in the Word of God that I haven't experienced yet. But today I'm going to teach you the pure, unadulterated Word of God. I want your faith to rest in the Word of God and not in the words or experiences of man. I will give you some personal examples to explain my points, but the main focus of this message in on God's Word. It is God's Word to you personally.

Here is what I tell people whenever I'm giving this message, "During the teaching of the Word, if you feel heat come all over your body or in the area of illness, if you feel electricity or tingling, or if you feel your pain lessening or moving then I want you to stand up. I'm just going to bless you in the Name of Jesus. After I acknowledge you and bless you then you may sit down." Now for you the reader: If while reading this, you start to feel any of these things that I have just mentioned, hold one of your hands out in front of you as an act of faith. I want you to receive what God is doing in your life as you read this message. Many times in the New Testament Jesus would tell people to do certain things as an act of faith. If the people responded with faith, then they would receive their healing. Just respond to His presence as you feel it upon you.

This book is not meant to give you more knowledge about God and His ways. This book is an invitation to experience the presence of God in a fresh way. It is an invitation for you to receive your healing. If we are only reading to get more knowledge, then we are falling short of what God has for us. We need to read this so that God can be unveiled to us and we can see Him in a fresh way. We need to read this as an invitation to our healing. So...be expecting today to receive from God!

{ Chapter 1 }

GUATEMALA

I went to Guatemala City and we met in a tent because they did not have a building yet. They had concrete floors where they were going to build later, but at the time they had a tent up over the concrete. It was as dusty inside of the tent as it was outside.

At the beginning of the message, I told the people what I have just explained to you. About five minutes into the sermon, a woman stood up to my right because she felt the anointing of God on her body. I had learned to say "Dios te bendiga," which means "God bless you" in Spanish. When she stood I looked at her and said "Dios te bendiga." As soon as I said that the power of God increased on her and she fell to the floor. She was down on the floor for the rest of the message.

At the end of the sermon, we had a time of impartation. Many people came forward, and the power of God was on them. There was a ten year old boy named Daniel. As I prayed for him, he fell to the floor and began to shake violently and cry. He was feeling the compassion of God for healing. Now, the woman who had fallen from the Presence earlier couldn't see any of this because she was still on the floor. When she got up some time later the Lord spoke to her and said, "Go to that boy and have him pray for you." In obedience to the Lord, she went to Daniel, and he prayed for her. Then the Lord spoke to her a second time and said, "Now go to the pastor's wife and have her pray for you." She had the pastor's wife pray for her, and she left the meeting.

The next day she came back to the meetings with her doctor's file in her hand and a testimony to share. She had been scheduled for a complete hysterectomy that very day, but postponed it because she wanted to come to the meeting. She had gone to her doctor that morning and said "Doctor, I won't let you operate on me till you give me another examination."

"I just gave you an examination the day before yesterday, you don't need another one," the doctor said.

"Yes, I do need another one because I feel like Jesus has healed me." She said.

The doctor was a skeptic who didn't believe in healing. He said, "Oh, come on...."

The woman's uterus had been completely full of tumors two days prior. The doctor examined her when she insisted. After her examination, he wrote on her chart,

> Not only were no tumors found, but the uterus appeared like the uterus of a twenty year old young woman.

This woman had the uterus of a twenty year old when in reality she was around forty years old! She brought the chart with her when she told us. God had completely healed this woman.

There have been other times when I would go through half of the sermon and nobody would stand up at all because nobody was sensing the presence of God working on their bodies. It happened like this when I was at Trinity International Church, an Assembly of God church in Lake Worth, Florida. Nothing seemed to happen during the first half of my message. All of a sudden, heaven was opened. It was hard to continue teaching because so many people were standing because they felt the anointing of God. God seemed to open heaven all at once!

Let's pray before we get into this message:

Lord, I ask for a holy expectation to come into every person reading this right now. I pray that they would not get so absorbed into reading and taking notes that they are not paying attention to their bodies. I ask for angels to come and superintend over every reader and give them an open heaven. I pray for them to come and touch the troubled waters – that those who would step into the water would be healed. I ask that You would release gifts of the Holy Spirit on every person right now. I pray there would be people sovereignly healed as we study the Word of God – that You would confirm Your Word with healings and manifestations of Your Spirit. I pray that every person would have the faith to hold out their hand in front of them as they feel Your presence come upon them – for all they are doing is responding to the instructions that if You sovereignly touch them, they would do this. It's a way of reaching out Lord, an act of faith. It's like when Jesus said, "Go, and dip in the pool." So Lord, I ask for healing to come for every person as they read this, in the Name of Jesus, Amen.

Now let us turn our attention to what the Word of God teaches pertaining to healing. This will not be an exhaustive study by any means. But it will be an attempt to begin to come to grips with many of the texts of the Bible that pertain to healing. Remember, I am not preaching my experiences, but rather what the Bible teaches about healing. My experience falls short of the Bible's teaching. My faith is in the Word of God and not my experiences. Let us look at the biblical foundation on the subject of healing.

{ Chapter 2 }

THE SELF REVELATION OF GOD AS HEALER

In the book of Exodus, God reveals His covenant keeping name, Jehovah-Rapha which means "the Lord who heals." At the beginning of the wilderness wanderings that lasted forty years, we see that God makes a covenant with the children of Israel. He says that if they walk in obedience, and do everything that He instructs, then none of the diseases which were allowed on the Egyptians will be allowed on them. God wanted to establish this early in their wanderings because He wanted them to know His provision of health and healing as they were going to be out in the wilderness for such a long period of time.

In Exodus 15:26b, the Lord says, "…for I am the Lord, who heals you." God is a God whose disclosure of Himself is as a God of healing. The name Jehovah-Rapha indicates that healing flows out from the nature of God. It is the very personality of God to bring healing and health to His covenant keeping people. It is God's heart to heal because that is who He is. We cannot separate healing from God. When something is part of our nature – then it is part of us. We cannot separate our nature from ourselves – our nature is who we are. It is our personality.

11

The same is true with God: you cannot separate who He is from what He does. You cannot separate His healing from who He is. He is a God who heals His people. Healing is His nature. You can't take that away from Him.

{ Chapter 3 }

HEALING AND THE PROPHETIC UNDERSTANDING OF THE MESSIAH

Healing was to be a prophetic indication for recognizing the Messiah when He came. It wasn't just to be how well He taught or what kind of principles He established. Rather, it was to be signs and wonders that validated the Messianic ministry. The Old Testament speaks extensively about this – especially in the Book of Isaiah. I want to take a look at two Scriptures in the Old Testament that show that one of the ways the Messiah was to be recognized was by His signs and wonders ministry.

> Strengthen the feeble hands, steady the knees that give way; say to those with fearful hearts, "Be strong, do not fear; your God will come, he will come with vengeance; with divine retribution he will come to save you." Then will the eyes of the blind be opened and the ears of the deaf unstopped. Then will the lame leap like a deer, and the mute tongue shout for joy. Water will gush forth in the wilderness and streams in the desert. (Isaiah 35:3-6)

Isaiah was speaking to the children of Israel when he declared this. He was telling them not to lose courage because there would be a time when God would come with power to save them from everything that was keeping them back from God's fullness in their lives. He was speaking of the day when the Messiah would come on the scene and change everything by what He does. Things would not be as they had always been. Isaiah points out that one of the ways that you will know when God is coming to save through His Messiah is when blind eyes begin to open, deaf ears begin to hear, lame people begin to leap, and the mute begin to shout for joy. The Messiah was to be recognized by the anointing that was upon His life for healing.

The second Scripture that I want to look at is Isaiah 61:1-2a:

> The Spirit of the Sovereign Lord is on me, because the Lord has anointed me to preach good news to the poor. He has sent me to bind up the brokenhearted, to proclaim freedom for the captives and release from darkness for the prisoners, to proclaim the year of the Lord's favor...

Isaiah was shown what the purpose of the Messiah would be when He came. The anointing of God was to be upon Him in a way that had not been seen up to that point. That anointing was to be manifested by preaching the good news to the poor as well as demonstrating the good news by power. God was sending a Messiah that would proclaim freedom to the prisoners and to heal those with broken hearts. Again, one of the ways that the Messiah was to be recognized was by the anointing on His life for healing.

Jesus confirms this by quoting these same Messianic prophecies relating them to Himself and His ministry to the sick and demonized. Now I want to look at two New Testament passages that are actually quotes from these two Old Testament scriptures that we looked at.

When Jesus began His ministry, He went on a forty day fast out in the wilderness and was tempted by the devil. After He overcame all the temptation that the enemy could bring against him during that season of His life, He returned to Galilee in the power of the Spirit. The first message that Jesus preached when He began His ministry is recorded in Luke 4:18-19. He quotes the passage from Isaiah 61 and says, "Today this scripture is fulfilled in your hearing." (Luke 4:21). He was saying, "I am the Messiah who was promised by God throughout the Old Testament Scriptures. My ministry will be characterized by the same anointing that you were expecting to be on the Messiah. Thus, I am the Messiah."

The next story is recorded in Luke chapter 7. John the Baptist was a man who was called by God to prepare the way for the Messiah's coming. He was to make the crooked places straight and the mountains and valleys into a level field so that God's Anointed One could come. He was the one prophet that was chosen by God to prepare the way for the Lord. He is the one that said, "Look, the Lamb of God, who takes away the sin of the world!" (John 1:29b).

He also said about Jesus, "He must become greater; I must become less." (John 3:30).

John was sure that Jesus was the Messiah and the fulfillment of God's promises in the Old Testament. God fulfilled the Word when He said, "The man on whom you see the Spirit come down and remain is he who will baptize with the Holy Spirit." (John 1:33). Everything that God had promised to John had happened. There was no reason for him to doubt that Jesus was the promised Messiah.

Later when John was in solitary confinement and all by himself, he began to doubt if Jesus was really the Messiah that was promised throughout the Old Testament. It's easy to have faith when you're popular and everybody is coming to you. Faith is a lot harder when you're isolated, spoken ill of, and put in a dungeon all by yourself. Jesus spoke highly of John the Baptist and respected him very much, yet John the Baptist was having a faith problem at this time. John sent men to Jesus to find out what was going on for sure. When the men came to Jesus, they said, "John the Baptist sent us to you to ask, 'Are you the one who was to come, or should we expect someone else'" (Luke 7:20).

Do I detect a wavering of faith there? Do I notice a bit of doubt in John the Baptist? The amazing thing is that he doesn't try to hide his doubt. He is being totally honest about it. He wants to be certain if this is the Messiah.

Now I want you to look at the response that Jesus gave. I think this is important to get because Jesus quotes again an Old Testament Messianic prophecy in relationship to Himself and His healing ministry. Jesus responds not just with words, but with actions as well:

> At that very time Jesus cured many who had diseases, sicknesses and evil spirits, and gave sight to many who were blind. So he replied to the messengers, 'Go back and report to John what you have seen and heard: The blind receive

sight, the lame walk, those who have leprosy are cured, the deaf hear, the dead are raised, and the good news is preached to the poor. Blessed is the man who does not fall away on account of me' (Luke 7:21-23).

It was through the words and actions of Jesus that John's faith was encouraged. Go back and show John what you have seen and heard. Healing was flowing through the ministry of Jesus, and the good news was preached. Jesus demonstrated and proclaimed the good news.

You can see that healing would be a prophetic indication for recognizing the Messiah. Jesus confirmed this many times by quoting Messianic prophecies in Isaiah 35 and 61, and relating them to Himself through His ministry to the sick and demonized.

I believe that there is the Body of the Messiah on earth today. His people who have been called out after Him and are in covenant with Him have the same anointing. We are His Body, and we get to partake of the same anointing He did while upon this earth. We are His expression on the earth today. We are His ambassadors that represent Him on the earth because we carry His authority. With that authority, we ought to see some of the same things happen in our time,

RANDY CLARK

{ Chapter 4 }

HE GIVES SIGHT TO THE BLIND

The meetings were exciting and every day was getting better than the day before. I would call my wife every night, and she would say, "I know, you're going to tell me that it is better tonight than it was last night."

My response was, "Well...Yes it was!"

In Cordoba Argentina, a woman received prayer for severe colon problems. When we prayed for her, she was healed, even though she was 66 years old at the time! She began to leave the meeting to go home, and we noticed that she was also blind, so we wanted to pray for that too. I asked her not to leave yet because we wanted to pray for her healing.

We asked the blind woman if we could pray for her. After interviewing her, we discovered she had been blind for three years. Her retina had been destroyed by diabetes. We began to pray for her and ended up praying for about an hour and a half. We prayed for her colon for about the first hour, and then started to pray for her eyes. About twenty minutes later her eyes began to feel warm. We told her, "That's good."

We felt like it was God's presence beginning to touch this

woman's eyes. After we prayed some more, she said "I think I can see a shadow."

There was a really big light in the field where we were, so I said, "Look at that light." I turned her head there and said, "Can you see me?"

"No."

"All right."

But we knew something was happening because of the warmth on her eyes. She kept saying, "I think I can see – it's getting lighter."

Excited, we kept on praying. A few minutes later she said, "I can see light." So we prayed some more and she said, "I can see forms." Encouraged by her improvement, we pressed in even more. We pulled her husband around in front of her and she said, "I can see! I see my husband!" You should've seen the look on her face!

I want you to know I had never seen a blind eye healed until 4 years ago. But since that time we have seen probably over 23 healed.[1] I've only had the privilege of praying for four of them myself-the rest of them were prayed for by members of the team that went with us on trips. They were just ordinary people like you and me. I will share a story about an ordinary person – a CPA in my church.

A CPA (Certified Public Accountant) from my church went with us to Chili and Argentina. We were traveling for about 15 days, and people's faith was beginning to rise. Since the CPA's faith had been increasing, he decided to pray for an older man that came forward for prayer. One of this man's eyes was totally destroyed, completely white with blindness, while the other eye was perfectly blue. On top of his blindness, he was also deaf in one ear. The CPA had never seen anybody healed in his life – at least no one that he personally prayed for. He prayed for this man. God touched the blind and deaf man, and he fell to the ground under the power of the Holy Spirit.

A lot of times when we pray for someone who falls to the ground, we go on praying for other people. We can't do that when it comes to praying for healing. When people fall over, it means that the anointing was so strong that they had a hard time standing up. We need to kneel down with them on the floor and ask them how they are doing and what they are feeling. Don't just walk off when someone falls. Just because someone falls to the ground doesn't mean that they are healed. We must try to get them to talk to us and find out what God is doing, because we only want to do what the Father is doing.

The CPA prayed for this man two or three times, and the man didn't feel anything happening. All of the sudden, as described in his own words, "I prayed one more time. He opened his eye and it was totally blue, and he could see. He could hear out of that ear that was deaf." All this took place around 3 or 4 in the morning. We ended up only getting 3-4 hours of sleep for this 15 nights, because of all the glorious things God did on that trip!

Later my CPA friend said to me, "Randy, I really realized how skeptical we are in North America. I prayed for that man. I had enough faith to pray for him, but when he got healed, here I am. I am the one that prayed for him. I saw it happen with my own eyes, and I'm lying here in bed saying, 'Did that really happen?' I'm telling you Randy, it is hard for me to believe – me personally – it's hard for me to believe that a man who was blind in his eye and deaf in his ear was healed, and I'm the one that God used to let the anointing flow through. That shows me, how much doubt and skepticism there really is in us North Americans."

There were some amazing things that happened when we went to Russia as well. One of the pastors with us was in his 60's. The father of one of the team members, he had a rare eye disorder and was declared legally blind. He already had three surgeries on his eyes and was preparing to have a fourth. His doctor knew he was going to Russia and said, "Well, we won't do the fourth surgery on you until after you go to Russia. If you come back and you're not healed, we'll do the surgery."

One night, with nobody praying for him, the Spirit of God came on him. He began to feel heat come into his eyes. When he got back to the room that night he opened up a book and started to read something that was in pinpoint type. He began to cry and say, "I can see! I can see that! I can read that!" He was so excited that God had healed him!

While we were in Moscow, a team member prayed for eight blind women. Four women were totally blind, and another four were legally blind, seeing only a few inches away. The power of God came that night as she began to pray for those eight women. Even though she had never seen a blind person healed before, she still prayed. Their eyes were opened! After being prayed for, one of the ladies who had been legally blind and could only see a few inches, looked clear across the room, which seated about 5,000 people. As she was looking she said, "That's my cousin. I remember what she looks like, and she has a barrette in her hair." I covered up my own contact that I use to see distances. I stood there looking, and I couldn't even see that far. It was truly a miracle of God!

1. These numbers are from the original printing of this manuscript in 2004. Since that time, we have seen hundreds of blind eyes open on our ministry trips. The majority of these occur when the team prays.

RANDY CLARK

{ Chapter 5 }

JESUS AND OUR COMMISSION TO HEAL

Healing was a sign to the people of the first century of the presence of the Messiah. Healing is also a sign of the Messiah's Body – His people who live in the earth today. To show you how important this was I want you to look again at Luke 4:18:

> The Spirit of the Lord is upon me because He has anointed me to preach Good News to the poor. He sent me to proclaim freedom for the prisoners, recovery of sight for the blind, to release the oppressed, and to proclaim the year of the Lord's favor.

Jesus was quoting this from Isaiah in reference to Himself. Healing was to be a sign of the anointing of God that rested on the Messiah. The Hebrew word for "Messiah" and the Greek word for "Christ" both mean the same thing – "the anointed one." Jesus is saying that He is the Anointed One that the prophet Isaiah was talking about. It was He that was going to bring healing and deliverance to hurting and broken people.

We are supposed to be anointed ones as well, because we are Christ's body here on earth. Healing, which is an indicator of the presence of the Messiah, should also be an indicator of the presence of the Messiah among His people today – His Body. My point is that we are not preaching the whole Gospel if we are leaving out the message of healing (see Romans 15:18, 19). The Gospel is not just about the forgiveness of sins, though that is a key element. Healing is not a side issue to the Good News of Jesus Christ. It is central to the Gospel. Christ came to bring healing to the whole person – body, soul and spirit. Healing has not been considered to be central by much of the Church today.

As a believers in Jesus the Messiah, you and I have been given a commission to pray for and to be used in healing the sick. It is not just for the elders of the Church to lay hands and be used to heal the sick. This is referenced in James 5:13-15:

> Is any one of you in trouble? He should pray. Is anyone happy? Let him sing songs of praise. Is any one of you sick? He should call the elders of the church to pray over him and anoint him with oil in the name of the Lord. And the prayer offered in faith will make the sick person well; the Lord will raise him up. If he has sinned, he will be forgiven.

This passage shows that we are to call for the elders to come and pray for us if we are sick. But I believe that this passage has been misunderstood for many years. I personally believe that this scripture is in reference to those who could not get to the gathering of God's people because their sickness was so bad. It is in this context that we are to call for the elders to come and anoint us with oil and pray for us. It isn't like the way we see it in our churches today, where the elders are the only ones in the Church Body who pray for the sick during ministry time, while everyone else sits and watches from the congregation. I think that it is fine to have the sick prayed for every week. But, we shouldn't limit praying to just the elders of the church.

In the church where I was pastor, we believed that every one of us has been commissioned to heal the sick. Because of this belief, we encouraged everyone to pray for the sick – not just the elders. So whether we're at church or at work, if someone is sick, we ought to be a light in the darkness and offer prayer for them. We should be asking God when we go to work, "God, let me be used at work today."

When I was teaching some time ago, a man came to the meeting who had a pretty important job at NASA. He told me a story wherein he went to work, and a guy came to him who was sick. So this man, believing that God could use him at his workplace, asked, "Can I pray for you?"

The sick man replied, "Yes," and even though he wasn't a churchgoer, he received prayer. He had never seen anything like this before. When he got prayer, the power of God came upon him, and he fell to the floor right in his workplace. He got up healed!

You might think that I'm telling you these stories because I'm a preacher. Well, I believe that anyone can pray for people anywhere – not just preachers. Let me tell you a story to illustrate this. It is not just preachers who can pray for the sick; it is all Christians.

When I started my former church, I took a job frying donuts for eleven months so that I could get to meet some people in the city of St. Louis. I traveled to over eighty Kroger stores in two states. I hated that job, but I knew God gave it to me for a purpose. I really knew it was a job God had given to me so I could be in St. Louis at least part of the time.

I would say, "Lord, You know I hate this job, and I thank You that You gave it to me. But it's so boring. Lord, if You would just let Your anointing come on me! If anybody says that they're sick, Lord, I'm going to pray for them. I am making a promise. This whole year that I'm frying donuts, if anybody at work tells me they are sick, I'm going to say, 'I'm a Christian, I believe that Jesus still heals today.'

When I would get the opportunity to pray for someone, I would tell them, "Now I can't promise you He's going to heal you. Some of the people that get prayer get healed, while others don't get healed. But I've seen many people get healed when we pray for them. Would you like me to pray for you?"

I wanted to see if it would work for anyone.

Ninety percent of the people I met were unbelievers. When I offered to pray for someone I was almost never turned down. Sadly, when you go to church today you get turned down by believers because they don't want you to pray for their healing. It is our commission to pray for the sick – every one of us.

I want to share another story from when I was frying donuts for those eleven months. I was a tech representative for Dawn Food Products. The head bakery clerk was acting really nervous one day so I went up to her and said, "You know, I don't even work for Kroger. I'm here to serve you. I'm here to help you and the people that are learning how to fry the donuts. So I'm just here to help you, don't be nervous."

"I'm not nervous because you're here," she said. "I'm nervous because I've had a severe infection in my ears, and I can hardly hear what you're saying. I'm nervous because I don't know what you're saying."

"Oh."

Later, I was over washing the dishes that I had used, and the thought came to me, "Are you going to pray for her?" Silently I said, "Yeah Lord, I told you I would."

So I went up to her and said, "You know, I'm a Christian, and I believe that Jesus still heals today... (All she knows is that I'm a donut fryer)... I can't promise you He's going to heal you, but if you would be willing, I will pray for you."

"I would like that."

"Well, when can I pray for you?

"Right now."

So we went back into the break room where there were about five other people smoking. That smoke was very heavy – and it definitely wasn't the Shekinah Glory.

Let me insert a thought here that I want to teach you on how you can do this naturally. We need to be able to become naturally supernatural. In Church, you can shout or use whatever style or mannerisms you want. In the workplace that's not going to be as effective. You have to learn how to naturally move in the supernatural – how to move in models of ministry that are transferable to outside the sanctuary. God sends us into the streets to do this stuff, not to keep it within the church. When we are a blessing, we will be well-spoken of. We keep saying, "Well, how am I going to witness to somebody?" Just look for a way of serving them and praying for them. Healing is a wonderful way to show the love of God to someone who is hurting.

When they don't know what to expect because of their lack of knowledge, I tell them this: "Listen, I'm not going to slap you on the head." That's important to say, because all some people have ever seen was something weird done on television. They're afraid you're going to do it to them. So I say, "I'm not going to slap you on the head, and I'm not going to yell at you. I'm going to pray with my eyes open and people are just going to think I'm talking to you. I don't want you to pray. You don't have to do anything. But if you begin to feel something, tell me."

So I asked this lady, "Is that OK?"

She said, "Yeah."

I put my hand up to her ear, and all I said was, "In the Name of Jesus" in the beginning of my prayer. All of the sudden she had a look of astonishment on her face. So I said, "You can hear?"

"Yes!" she shouted. You should've seen her face. I didn't even get to pray anything. She said, "As soon as you said 'In the Name of Jesus,' my ear popped open."

Now that she just had an encounter with Jesus, it is easy to make the next transition. Healing is a great way to transition to ask someone about their relationship with God. I asked her, "Well, how do you feel about Jesus?"

She began to cry and sob as she told me that "Several years ago I was on the Session of the Presbyterian Church. I got really hurt and I've not been back to that church since that day."

"Well, how do you feel about God now?"

Still weeping she said, "I didn't think He would touch me."

"Do you feel His love?"

"Yes."

"Well, why don't you go back and forgive them, and tell them what He did for you." She went back and explained what had happened and got involved in church once again. God moved powerfully on that woman in the break room, right in the midst of other people and the cigarette smoke.

Moving in the supernatural in the work place makes the Christian life fun. It's what makes work tolerable. There is an element of surprise as you go into work everyday, because you don't know when you are going to step into the supernatural. If the only time that God can work is when we meet together for church, then we have God in a very small box. He wants to use each of us to be a blessing in the community that we are in. Almost none of my testimonies that first year came from being at church; rather they came

from being at work.
I said, "Well God, how come there is so much faith in the work place?"

His response was this: "Because they have not been taught that I don't do anything." Pagans believe if there is a God, He has power. Those who have gone some place where they have been taught that God stopped doing signs and wonders don't have much expectation.

I asked this one man, "Can I pray for you?"

He said, "No." It is one of the few times that I got turned down.

"Well, why not?"

"If you pray for me, I know that God is going to change me, and I don't want to change."

Did he have faith? Yes, he had a lot of faith. What he didn't have was repentance with his faith. It is not enough to believe – "even the demons believe and tremble." (James 2:19b).

{ Chapter 6 }

GOD HAS COMMISSIONED ALL CHRISTIANS TO HEAL

Every one of us is commissioned to heal the sick. This is Jesus' commission to his disciples when He was upon the earth, and it is His commission to us today. In Matthew 10:7-8, Jesus charges His disciples, saying:

> As you go, preach this message: 'The kingdom of heaven is near.' Heal the sick, raise the dead, cleanse those who have leprosy, drive out demons. Freely you have received, freely give.

You can see that Jesus commissioned His disciples to work signs and wonders, as well as preach the Gospel. Just as Jesus went about teaching, preaching, and healing (Mt. 4:23), so His disciples were to go around doing the same. The disciples were to have the same ministry that Jesus had. There are some people who believe that I'm not treating the scriptures properly because I say that. They think that you cannot apply to every believer what Jesus only spoke to the disciples. Let me show you how this is not true.

Jesus' words to His disciples were many. If we cut out everything that He said to only them, then we would not have much of the Gospels left. So you cannot say that

Jesus' words were just for the twelve Apostles, who walked and talked with Him. These words are for every one of us throughout the rest of time. If one thing doesn't apply to us, then none of what Jesus taught can apply to us. We cannot pick and choose what we want out of the Bible and say that the rest of it was never intended for us. Either all of it is for us, or none of it is for us.

All of us have a commission to heal that was given to us by Jesus Himself. Let us look at another scripture; Mark 6:7, 12-13 says:

> Calling the Twelve to him, he sent them out two by two and gave them authority over evil spirits…They went out and preached that people should repent. They drove out many demons and anointed many sick people with oil and healed them.

Again, we have Jesus commissioning His disciples to preach the Gospel and to evangelize the world. He gave them a command to go out two by two to complete this task. But it says that as they went out they preached that people should repent and turn from the way of life that they had been living in. Accompanied with this proclamation of the Gospel, there was a demonstration of it as well. While they were preaching repentance to the people, they were demonstrating it by bringing deliverance to the demonized and anointing with oil many who were sick.

My point is that deliverance and healing were just as essential to the Gospel as the actual proclamation of the message. Maybe you are still thinking this is just for the twelve disciples that physically walked with Jesus on the earth. Let me share one more scripture to build my point a little further.

Let us look at Matthew 28:19-20. Jesus is again speaking to the disciples and he says to them:

Therefore go and make disciples of all nations, baptizing them in the name of the Father and of the Son and of the Holy Spirit, and teaching them to obey everything I have commanded you. And surely I am with you always, to the very end of the age.

This is what many call the Great Commission. You can talk to almost anyone today, and they will tell you that this is just as applicable to us as it was to the disciples of Jesus. The disciples were to pass Jesus' teachings on to the next generation, and that generation would do the same. This passage is for us just as much as it was for the people of Jesus' day. We are to receive the teachings of Jesus then pass them on to others.

Part of the teachings of Jesus include healing and deliverance. The ministry of Jesus was not relegated to the forgiveness of sins. It was to bring healing to the total person – body, soul and spirit. If it doesn't bring freedom to all of these areas then it is not the same Gospel that Jesus preached and demonstrated while He walked on this earth.

Did you know you have been commissioned? You have been anointed by God, and with that anointing came a commission. Most of us have not understood that the anointing brings a charge. The anointing comes so that we can fulfill the commission with the Holy Spirit's power. The task that was given to us is greater than we can do by ourselves. It can only be accomplished by the Spirit's power. When we accepted the Lordship of Jesus Christ and as Savior, we accepted a responsibility. We are the ones, in this world, who have an anointing. Because of this anointing we should at least offer to pray for the sick and the lost.

{ Chapter 7 }

THE SCOPE OF HEALING

Now that we know we are commissioned to heal, what can we say about the scope of healing? Is healing for everyone, or for a few chosen people? To what extent does God heal? Does He heal every disease or just a few different types of diseases?

There are some people who could be accused of having a Bible within the Bible. They say that they don't believe some of the Bible is for today, but they believe that other parts of it are for today. There are some people who have a very narrow scope on how much God heals today. They believe that God can heal headaches but not cancer. They believe God can take away physical illness, but they do not believe He can heal mental illness. These people think God is limited in who and what He can heal.

There was a time when I believed that God could heal physically, but I had some trouble believing that He could heal mental illnesses. We had a support group at our church for the mentally ill in which you had to have been diagnosed with some form of mental illness in order to get into the group. The group was very large because there wasn't a group like that in the community. We had those with a wide range of problems like schizophrenia, bipolar disorder, etc. At one point, I was afraid that those of us who were not mentally ill were going to be outnumbered by those who were. I ended up becoming very close with many of them – they were my dear friends. I would go and visit them in the hospital. It was hard to see them suffering so much. Though, it was really neat to see how well they understood each other. When one was hospitalized, all of them would come and be a support group to the one.

In that group was a man named Dennis who was diagnosed with schizophrenia. For several years, I would pray for him every time that I saw him at church. While in a severely depressed state he tragically died of what appeared to be an accidental overdose. I had been crying out to God for years to see Him heal the mentally ill. While crying out to God I said, "God, I have expectations for physical illness, but I haven't seen mental illness healed yet. I honestly have very little expectation for it." I must confess that I did not have much faith for healing schizophrenia until recently. But seeing Dennis die of this mental illness made me press into God with a greater force than if I hadn't experienced it.

During March of 1999, I was ministering in Cordoba, Argentina with Omar Cabrera, Jr. While I was there, I was introduced to a woman who had been extremely debilitated by a severe form of schizophrenia. At one point in her life, she was about to be admitted to a hospital where almost no one was ever released. She told me how she visited one of Omar Cabrera, Sr.'s meetings and was instantly healed of her schizophrenia. No one even prayed for her that day. She was healed as she entered the Church, while the people were worshipping God.

Now, it is one thing to believe that God can heal, and it is another thing to have expectation that God is going to heal. Believing that God can heal is an intellectual faith that says, "I believe intellectually that God can heal today." That is different than expecting Him to heal in the service you are in right then or where you are at right now. Ask Him to heal you. Believe that He will and then begin acting on it.

Next I want to talk about the extent of healing. Psalm 103:2-3 reads:

> Praise the Lord, O my soul,
> and forget not all his benefits—
> who forgives all your sins
> and heals all your diseases...

David is telling us that in the midst of our praise we are not to forget any of the things that God provides for us. Two of the benefits that David lists are the forgiveness of sins and the healing of diseases. Now, how many of us believe God forgives us all of our sins? I think that most of us would agree that if we confess our sins, than God will be faithful to forgive us. Why do you believe it? We believe it because the Bible says so (I John 1:9). But we must remember that while it says He forgives all our sins, it also says He heals all our diseases.

We need to understand that this is the Word of God, so it must be true. However, not everyone in the world gets saved and forgiven of their sins. All sins can be forgiven if they are confessed – there is no sin that God cannot wipe away and cleanse.

There is something that I don't understand though. The Spirit of God can move over a building. People come forward weeping because they are lost or backslidden, and deeply convicted of their sin. It is a gift of God. When the Spirit of the Living God arrives, some weep, but another one laughs, while the rest sit there thinking, "Well, I'm not feeling anything." This is the sovereignty of God.

In the same way, God can heal all of our sicknesses and all of our diseases. But not everyone gets healed of everything. Just because everyone doesn't get healed however, doesn't mean that God doesn't heal today. I don't fully understand why everyone doesn't get healed, and I don't have definitive answers. I will suggest one reason in a later chapter.

I would like to talk about the fullness of the scope of healing. God's healing power can touch every type of disease and sickness. Let us say you come up to me and say, "I've got cancer. Do you have enough faith to pray for that?"

My answer is, "I can't heal your cancer. I can't heal a toothache. I can't heal a headache. I don't have enough faith in me to heal anything. But the same God who heals a toothache and a headache, is the same God who heals cancer." My faith is not in me; my faith rests in God alone. He is the only one who can heal somebody. He wants to operate through you to heal the sick and deliver those that are demonized.

Heather Harvey, a 14-year-old girl, came up for healing of dyslexia. When we prayed for her, she fell to the floor and remained there for quite some time. When she got up, she felt cold, like her body temperature had dropped. While on the floor, she had a vision of angels coming, opening her head up, and rewiring her brain. The angels put everything back together. She was healed that night! Her Mom and Dad were mental health professionals before they entered the ministry. I've checked with her every year since then, and she is still healed!

When Heather went home, she did not tell her best friend Monica (who had dyslexia also) what had happened to her. Monica's parents were educators and also associate pastors. When she got home she went to Monica's house and said, "Monica, the Lord Jesus is going to heal you." After she said this, she put her hands on Monica's head and Monica fell to the floor under the power of the Spirit and had a vision. She saw angels come and operate on her head, rewire her brain, and then it was over. Monica was also healed of dyslexia!

We were in Greensboro, North Carolina, in a Vineyard that used to be a Presbyterian Church. A small school-aged boy with ADD came up to me with his Mom. At the time, I didn't even know what ADD or ADHD was. On top of that, I had never prayed for someone who had ADD before. But I know that the Bible says that God heals all diseases-not just physical diseases, all diseases. We laid our hands on him and prayed.

Six months later, we were in High Point, North Carolina, and the boy's mother came up to me. She said, "Remember that night you prayed for my son?"

"Yeah, I remember that."

"The school teacher sent a note home the next day and asked, 'What happened to your son? He was tested and doesn't have ADD anymore.'"

In Florence, Kentucky we prayed for a little girl who had been diagnosed by a psychiatrist as borderline sociopathic and needed to be institutionalized. She was a little girl who had been adopted 2 years earlier from Russia. We prayed for her, and God moved in a wonderful way. When I went back three months later, her mother reported, "We took her back to the doctor and she tested normal."

God heals every type of sickness and disease. If you are sick, there is hope for you. You don't have a sickness too big for God to heal. He has power to heal, and He has a desire to heal you!

{ Chapter 8 }

THE BASIS FOR HEALING

Now that we have looked at the scope of healing, let us turn our attention to the basis of healing. What can we base our healing on? Can we base it on the Word of God? If we can base it on the Word of God, then what is it that the Word lays out for us?

The Covenant

The first foundation in the Word of God upon which we can support our healing is the Covenant that God made with His people. God declares in Exodus 34:10:

> I am making a covenant with you. Before all your people I will do wonders never before done in any nation in all the world. The people you live among will see how awesome is the work that I, the Lord, will do for you.

God established a covenant with the children of Israel. Signs and wonders are to be part of the establishment of that covenant. The word 'wonders' in this text means "miraculous things in nature." But a miracle doesn't have to be just in nature. Rather, God did wonderful things in the hearts and in the bodies of the people. Healing and deliverance are included in 'signs and wonders.' But 'signs and wonders' are more than healings and deliverances. The Bible says if we obey this covenant that He established, then we will not have the sicknesses that were on the people of Egypt.

So we see that healing is part of the Covenant God made with us. Healing was in the Old Covenant, and the book of Hebrews says that we have a better Covenant based upon a better sacrifice, with better promises. Healing is in the New Covenant. When we celebrate the Lord's Supper, I know its power is not only available for grace to cover our sins, but also for grace that enables us to have victory over diseases.

I learned something more about the power of the Lord's Supper when we visited Harold Cabelleros's church in Guatemala. He told me about a person who found a curse that a witch or warlock had put on a particular house. As a result of the curse, the people who lived in the house were constantly sick. They went to another witch who examined it and said he could tell that the person who put the curse on it had a higher power than he did. So he said, "I cannot break the power of that curse because you need to have somebody who has a higher power. The pact that they made is stronger than my power. You have to go to a witch with stronger authority than the one who made this curse in order to break it."

I thought, "Oh man! I know a covenant that is more powerful than any witch or warlock's pact." It's the pact from Luke 22 that I mention every time I stand up on Sunday morning saying:

> On the night that our Lord was betrayed, He took the bread and He gave it to His disciples and said,

'This is My body which was given for you.' And likewise after the supper He took the cup and He blessed it, and He gave it to his disciples and said, 'This cup is a New Covenant. In My blood which was shed for many, for the remission of sins, drink ye all of it, for as often as you eat of this bread and drink of this cup, you proclaim the Lord's death until He comes.'

There is more power in that pact, more power in the New Covenant than there is in the curses others may want to put on us. Healing is in the Covenant. Not only is it in the Covenant, but it is also in the Atonement.

The Atonement

Isaiah 53:4-5 says:

Surely he took up our infirmities and carried our sorrows, yet we considered him stricken by God, smitten by Him, and afflicted. But he was pierced for our transgressions, he was crushed for our iniquities; the punishment that brought us peace was upon him, and by his wounds we are healed.

Let us take a look at the first part of verse 4; 'infirmities' and 'sorrows' can be rendered as diseases and physical sickness. We make a mistake when we say that Isaiah 53 refers just to forgiveness of sins or spiritual healing. We make the same mistake if we think that it refers just to physical healing. The fact is that Christ came to redeem the whole man through the Atonement – body, soul, and spirit. It is not that you have to choose one above the other; it is both. This passage is referring to spiritual healing as well as physical healing.

Christ came to heal every area of sickness in every person. That is the basis of healing.

Matthew confirmed that this Isaiah passage refers to physical healing when he wrote his gospel under the inspiration of the Holy Spirit:

> When evening came many who were demon possessed were brought to Him. And He drove out the spirits with a word, and He healed all the sick. This was to fulfill what was spoken by the prophet Isaiah: 'He took up our infirmities and carried our diseases.' (Matthew 8:16-17)

The Holy Spirit inspired this. The Holy Spirit knew what He meant when He spoke through Isaiah. Matthew says one of the reasons Jesus went about healing people's sicknesses and delivering people from demonic forces was to fulfill what the Spirit spoke through Isaiah: 'He took up our infirmities and carried our diseases.'

Physical healing is in the Atonement. I don't understand this, but I know that everything good we receive from God comes by His grace and His mercy. This could be given to us because He knew in the midst of time there would be a Cross upon which His only begotten Son would die. Everything that is good comes in the Atonement. In the Atonement, the grace of God is made available to us for the forgiveness of sins and the healing of the body.

Peter refers to the Isaiah 53 passage by relating it to forgiveness of sins. 1 Peter 2:24 says, "By His stripes we were healed." I know that I've said this before. But let me say it again: All healing comes through the Atonement.

Whether we need forgiveness of sins, mental healing, or any type of physical healing – it was provided through the Atonement.

There is never any basis for healing promised to us through the scriptures based on what we have or haven't done. So never ask for someone's healing based on his or her merit, no matter how good they are or what they have done. Why would we offer to God, "Would you heal him because of what he has done?" Jesus, His only begotten Son, died on a Cross. If we have faith that God ought to heal, it is not because we are good, but because His Son died. He left Heaven and came to the earth to die. That is the basis by which we have a covenant with God; God entered into a Covenant with us. There's one more reason, and I pray on the basis of all three:

1) God, I want to remind you of your Covenant. God, I remind You of Your Covenant with better promises, based on a better sacrifice.
2) God, I ask you to heal this man or this woman because of what Jesus did. Lord, I ask you to heal because of the Atonement. He died, He bore in His Body our diseases and sicknesses.
3) Lord, I ask you to heal because in the Kingdom of God there is healing. The kingdom is both now and not yet. The kingdom is here, but not fully consummated. And that is a possible reason why not everyone gets healed every time we pray.

The Kingdom of God

Let us turn to Luke 10:9. I want this to be the foundational text for healing being in the Kingdom of God. When Jesus was commissioning His disciples He told them, "Heal the sick who are there and tell them, 'The kingdom of God is near you.'" Healing is in the Kingdom of God, and in the Kingdom of God there is healing.

We pray the Lord's prayer, "Our Father who art in Heaven, hallowed be thy Name, thy kingdom come and thy will done on earth as it is in Heaven..." We declare it. Is there any sickness or disease in Heaven? No. Then we know what the ultimate will of the Father is. The will of God is that healing take place on the earth. When we are praying for the Kingdom of God to come and His will to be done, then we need to look to heaven as a model for earth. If it doesn't exist in heaven, then it doesn't have to exist on earth. Heaven should be our model of ministry.

In Revelations 21:4, Jesus says, "...There will be no more death or mourning or crying or pain, for the old order of things have passed away." We know when He comes we shall be like Him because we're going to see Him as He is (1 John 3:2). When we get to heaven, God is going to give us the same type of glorified body that He gave his Son. This is not going to happen while on earth because His kingdom is not fully here and will never be fully here until Jesus comes back. That time when everybody is healed and there will be no sickness among us is not going to happen until Jesus comes back in His second coming. Until then, there is an ebb and flow to the healing ministry – it is a mystery. There is the in-break of the Kingdom of God into our lives. It is a Kingdom that is both now and not yet – a Kingdom in which we may only be experiencing in part, but always be pressing in for more of the "now."

That night in Cordoba Argentina, when within fifteen minutes 800 people got healed, we had a visitation of the in-break of the Kingdom. My desire is that the people of God would get a vision for what it is like when the Shekinah Glory comes in. I remember one morning God woke me up from a deep sleep. There was a thought that went through my head. I knew it was the Lord and wrote it down. He said, "When My presence is amongst you in worship, My presence is with you for healing." God's kingdom is among us when His presence is manifest in our worship.

In Luke 10:9, Jesus commissions the seventy-two and tells them, "Heal the sick who are there and tell them, 'The kingdom of God is near you.'" Now there is a real danger here of being misunderstood, because we can logically deduct that, "If the kingdom of God is in me, and healing is in the kingdom, then healing is in me, and I can heal people." But you have to interpret scripture by scripture, right? Healing is in the kingdom, but the kingdom has a King and I am not that King. I am part of the kingdom – not the whole kingdom and not in charge of the kingdom.

I want to look at Luke 17:20-21:

> Once, having been asked by the Pharisees when the kingdom of God would come, Jesus replied, "The kingdom of God does not come visibly, nor will people say, 'Here it is,' or 'There it is,' because the kingdom of God is within you."

We don't want to be like the people who practice New Age. What do they teach? "The ground of all being is everywhere and in everything (a kind of pantheism). It's in you, and what you need to do is release the power in you."

We have to be very careful lest we begin to think the same

way, "I've got the kingdom in me, so I can release the power through me when I want to." It may be logical, but it is not biblical. God is still the King, and He is the one who heals.

{ Chapter 9 }

PETER, AN EXAMPLE OF HOW TO MINISTER HEALING

Now we are going to look at Acts 3:1-2:

> One day Peter and John were going up to the temple at the time of prayer, at three in the afternoon. Now a man crippled from birth was being carried to the temple gate called Beautiful, where he was put every day to beg from those going into the temple courts.

I want to interject here that Jesus had walked by that man before when He went to the Temple. Everyday that man was brought to that gate. Jesus must have walked by him. Did you know Jesus walked into a hospital one time and only healed one person and walked out? That was at the pool of Bethesda. Because that's the only one the Father said to heal. He said, "I do nothing of myself, I can do only what I see the Father doing" (John 5: 19).

Peter and John had gone to the temple day by day and they had walked by that man many times. Let's read from Acts 3: 3-11:

> When he saw Peter and John about to enter, he asked them for money. Peter looked straight at

him, as did John. Then Peter said, 'Look at us!'
So the man gave them his attention, expecting to
get something from them. Then Peter said, 'Silver
and gold I do not have, but what I have I give you.
In the name of Jesus Christ of Nazareth walk.'
Taking him by the right hand, he helped him up,
and instantly the man's feet and ankles became
strong. He jumped to his feet and began to walk.
Then he went with them into the temple court
walking and jumping, and praising God. When
all the people saw him walking and praising God,
they recognized him as the same man who used
to sit begging at the temple gate called Beautiful,
and they were filled with wonder and amazement
at what happened to him. While the beggar
held on to Peter and John, all the people were
astonished and came running to them in the place
called Solomon's Colonnade.

Peter had a choice here: he could take the glory for himself
or he could point the people to Christ. He could have said,
"Oh man, you should've seen me. I had such a powerful
word of knowledge. I mean, it was so strong, and oh the
power of God came through me..." I want to be like Peter in
this situation, and I hope you would too.

Peter was the first Teflon® Christian, and we ought to be
Teflon® Christians as well. If we aren't Teflon® Christians,
the enemy will destroy us. Teflon® is a substance that creates
a non-stick surface. When God does show up, and when the
praise comes, you won't let it stick to you. You will point
beyond yourself to the one who really did the healing – to
Christ.

Now continuing in Acts 3:12:

> When Peter saw this, he said to them, 'Men of
> Israel, why does this surprise you? Why do you
> stare at us as if by our own power or godliness we
> had made this man walk?'

Peter was saying that is wasn't how devoted he was to God
that made this man whole. He wasn't saying it was by his
own godliness or power. He was pointing the way to Jesus.
We have to remember it is not our power or godliness that
heals people.

Then he preaches to them the story of Jesus and the good
news. In Acts 3:16, Peter proclaims:

> But by faith in the name of Jesus, this man whom
> you see and know was made strong. It's Jesus'
> Name and the faith that comes through Him that
> has given this complete healing to him even as
> you now see.

In Acts 4, Peter and John are now before the Sanhedrin. The
men of the Sanhedrin are upset because this man has been
healed. They don't like it because the miracle drew a large
crowd. And the people were asking, "How was this done?"
This gave an opportunity for Peter and John to preach to
them and tell them the reason the man was healed.

> Then know this you and all the people of Israel,
> it's by the name of Jesus Christ of Nazareth
> whom you crucified, but whom God raised from
> the dead that this man stands before you healed.
> (Acts 4:10).

What they are saying is that this wasn't them. They were pointing to the one who heals. It is not our godliness or power, but it is faith in the name of Jesus (Acts 3:16). He is the healer. He is the one who was crucified. He is the anointed one. It is Him through whom we have a covenant. It is through His Atonement that we have this covenant, and it is in His kingdom. The entire basis for healing is in Him.

Now I want to conclude this point with this: You have to be like Peter. At first, when you begin to move in more anointing and success in healing, the devil will tell you He doesn't heal any more. If God heals, he will tell you that you did it. So you must know it's not you. It is not you or me. I really make efforts when sharing testimonies to say it wasn't me.

God can use little ol' me! Now that is not to say that there are not some people God sovereignly chooses to give a ministry of healing to. All of us are commissioned, just like we are all commissioned to share our faith. But there are some who are evangelists who will share their faith a lot more than the average Christian. All are commissioned to pray for the sick, and there are some who have stronger anointing in the gift and ministry of healing. But that does not release any of us from the Great Commission.

I believe that I have failed as a pastor if I have not instructed my people to understand that it is mandatory for us as Christians to share our faith, pray for the sick and learn how to cast out demons. That is the basis of the Gospel, not peripheral to it. If we focus and have more success in that, then our churches would be bursting with people coming in. Church would be a place they could come and get free. Church would be the place for healing. I want to see that in the Body of Christ.

{Chapter 10}

THE MYSTERY OF HEALING

Healing cannot be reduced to a formula, to a prayer technique, or to controlling God somehow by His own Word. God is the Sovereign One, and we are His servants. It is never the other way around. The Bible is rich with great and wonderful promises. But in the midst of the world of the supernatural where miracles are occurring, there is the mystery of those who do not get healed. This mystery is found not only in the life around us but also in the Holy Bible. Jesus and the Apostle Paul had to learn to live with this mystery of healing, and so must we.

We find that in the ministry of Jesus and Paul there were times when the anointing was greater for healing. There were also times when the anointing was lower for healing. Let us look at an example from the ministry of Jesus and from the ministry of Paul to further illustrate this point.

Greater Anointing for Healing

At times the anointing is greater for healing. The last part of Luke 5:17 declares, "And the power of the Lord was present for him to heal the sick." I believe that Jesus, the eternal Son of God, clothed His omnipotent power in humility. He chose to be dependent totally upon the Holy Spirit, defeating the enemies of God, the devil and disease in his humanity. This happened in order for us to be able to identify with Him, for Him to defeat Satan as a man, and so that He could be the second Adam – our Federal head and representative.

This passage indicates that there were times when the "power of the Lord was present for him to heal the sick" and times when it wasn't as manifest to heal people. That is the mystery of healing.

Let us look at an example from the Apostle Paul. Acts 19:11 says, "God did extraordinary miracles through Paul...." There were times when God did 'extraordinary miracles' through Paul. At other times God did not do them. Let us take a look at two examples where the anointing wasn't as strong for healing in the life of Jesus and the life of Paul.

Lesser Anointing for Healing

Let us look at a passage from Mark:

> Jesus said to them, 'Only in his hometown, among his relatives and in his own house is a prophet without honor.' He could not do any miracles there, except lay his hands on a few sick people and heal them. And he was amazed at their lack of faith. (Mark 6:4-6)

As you can see from Jesus' life, he had a time when the anointing was greater, and the power of the Lord was present for healing. Then we see in this passage that the anointing was lesser for healing because of the people's unbelief.

This is not intended as an encouragement to pass judgment on someone when they are not healed, or the anointing is lower for healing. Our job is not to tell someone that they don't have enough faith. That actually discourages them instead of encouraging them. If you feel they don't have enough faith to be healed, you should encourage them with Scriptures that they can meditate on to build their faith. Our job is to press in for more anointing in the healing arena when people are not healed. The earlier example is simply a further illustration that Jesus also operated in varying levels of anointing.

Here is another scripture that shows that Paul operated in a lesser anointing for healing at times as well. Let us look at 2 Timothy 4:20, "Erastus stayed in Corinth, and I left Trophimus sick in Miletus." Here we have the mystery of the Apostle Paul who had seen even handkerchiefs bring healing to the sick in Ephesus, now having to leave one of his apostolic team members sick in Miletus.

This just shows not everyone is healed when we pray for them. We are not to condemn ourselves when everyone is not healed. Rather, we are to press in for more of God. We can't blame ourselves or the people we are praying for when people don't get healed.

The Apostle Paul was not being rhetorical when he stated in 1 Corinthians 13 that he only "knew in part." We may not understand the mystery of healing, but we should have a proper motive for healing. Let us look at what I believe was a guiding motive for the ministry of the Apostle Paul.

RANDY CLARK

{Chapter 11}

THE MOTIVE FOR HEALING

What is the motive for healing? I've thought about the motive for healing many times. I thought it could be compassion or it could be the love of God motivating us to pray for healing. There are many motivations when it comes to praying for the sick. We often feel love and compassion for our friends and families much more than the poor stranger at our door. For even our love and compassion is contaminated by our selfishness. Let us look at what I believe should be the human motive in praying for healing.

That motive is found in Acts 19:17b. This is right in the middle of the greatest revival Paul ever had in the city Ephesus, the city where the greatest healings took place. Paul stayed in Ephesus for two years and did extraordinary miracles in the name of Jesus.

The Jewish exorcists who used the name of Jesus were attacked and fled bleeding and naked. The demon had answered them, "Jesus I know, and I know about Paul, but who are you?" (Acts 19:15). Verse 17 goes on to declare:

> When this became known to the Jews and the
> Greeks living in Ephesus, they were all seized

with fear and the Name of the Lord Jesus was held in high honor.

Often in my prayers for the sick, I say, "God touch this man, that Your Name, the Name of your Son Jesus would be held in high honor in (and I name the city), that the name Jesus would no longer be a swear word on the lips of many, but you would move in such power that it would even become a praise word. I ask for healing that the Name of Jesus would be held in high honor." Our motive must always be to honor the name of Jesus Christ in our midst.

{Chapter 12}

A PRAYER FOR YOUR HEALING

Now I would like to encourage any of you who have need of healing to read the following prayer through twice, and then pray it forming the words with your lips – not as a silent prayer. If you are in a public place like a library or somewhere else where you can't talk out loud, just offer the following prayer in a soft whisper.

When you are praying and you see the dots on the page, you should wait before continuing with the prayer. While you are waiting, focus on your body with expectation that God may touch you. You may feel the pain diminishing, feel heat, electricity, coolness, or a combination thereof, or you may feel nothing except that you begin to notice that the area of sickness or pain is being healed. If you do sense some of the phenomena just mentioned, let it encourage you, as these are often indications of the anointing for healing. You may want to wait a minute or so each time you see the dots on the page. I would encourage you to wait in silence – not saying anything but waiting with expectation, giving God the opportunity to touch you. Now, let's pray.

Father, I thank You for Your anointing. I pray God that more healing would take place, even now as I'm holding my hand(s) out in front of me.

....

That what I held my hand out for earlier when I felt Your anointing, and as it is continuing now, I pray in Jesus' Name for more healing power to flow through me.

....

In Jesus' name, let Your anointing get even stronger. I receive and bless what You're doing now, in the Name of Jesus.

....

God, thank you for Your healing power that is flowing through me right now. I command sickness and disease to leave in the Name of Jesus Christ of Nazareth.

....

I speak healing in Your Name to flow through my body that every symptom would leave. In Jesus Name I command the pain to leave now.

....

In Jesus Name, I ask You to increase the anointing. Increase it, Lord. More Lord in the Name of Jesus.

....

Not because I'm worthy. I look to the Cross. All of my hope is in the Cross, and what You did. Thank You Lord, In Jesus' Name Amen.

If you have received healing while reading this book, please write your testimony down, and send it to me at my office.

The email address is goglobal@globalawakening.com.

Or you can send it to the following address:
Global Awakening
1451 Clark Street
Mechanicsburg, PA 17055

Other books by Randy Clark

Entertaining Angels

There Is More

Power, Holiness and Evangelism

Lighting Fires

God Can Use Little Ole Me

Other Booklets by Randy Clark

Evangelism Unleashed

Healing Ministry and Your Church

Learning to Minister Under the Anointing

Training Manuals Available

Ministry Team Training Manual

Schools of Healing and Impartation Workbooks

Core Message Series

Words of Knowledge

Biblical Basis of Healing

Baptism in the Holy Spirit

Open Heaven

Pressing In

The Thrill of Victory / The Agony of Defeat

Awed by His Grace / Out of the Bunkhouse

In "There Is More", Randy lays a solid biblical foundation for a theology of impartation as well as taking a historical look at impartation and visitation of the Lord in the Church. This is combined with many personal testimonies of people who have received an impartation throughout the world and what the lasting fruit has been in their lives. You are taken on journey throughout the world to see for yourself the lasting fruit that is taking place in the harvest field - particularly in Mozambique. This release of power is not only about phenomena of the Holy Spirit, it is about its ultimate effect on evangelism and missions. Your heart will be stirred for more as you read this book.

"This is the book that Randy Clark was born to write."
- Bill Johnson

GLOBAL SCHOOL OF SUPERNATURAL MINISTRY

Vision

To release followers of Christ into their specific destiny and calling, in order to live out the Great Commission.

Structure

Global School of Supernatural Ministry is a one or two year ministry school with an emphasis on impartation and equipping students for a life of walking in the supernatural. Classes start each September and end the following May. Courses are offered on-site at the Apostolic Resource Center in Mechanicsburg, PA. Upon completion of each program year a Certificate of Completion is awarded. Students seeking additional educational training may do so while attending GSSM through the Wagner Leadership Institute.

Community

The GSSM student body is diverse in age, culture, ministry experience, and educational accomplishments. From high school graduates to professionals to retirees - the students come together seeking more of God. Supernatural power, passion and honor are key values of GSSM and are reflected in our worship, outreach and personal relationships.

For more information - or to enroll in classes - contact us at
1-866-AWAKENING or apply online at
http://gssm.globalawakening.com

globalawakening

For a schedule of upcoming events and conferences, or to purchase other products from Global Awakening, please visit our website at:

http://www.globalawakening.com